KILLER ANIMALS
ANACONDAS
ON THE HUNT

by Lori Polydoros

Reading Consultant:
Barbara J. Fox
Reading Specialist
North Carolina State University

Content Consultants:

Joe Maierhauser, President/CEO
Terry Phillip, Curator of Reptiles
Reptile Gardens
Rapid City, South Dakota

Robert T. Mason, PhD
Professor of Zoology
J.C. Braly Curator of Vertebrates
Oregon State University, Corvallis

Capstone
press

Mankato, Minnesota

Blazers is published by Capstone Press,
151 Good Counsel Drive, P.O. Box 669, Mankato, Minnesota 56002.
www.capstonepress.com

Copyright © 2010 by Capstone Press, a Capstone Publishers company.
All rights reserved.
No part of this publication may be reproduced in whole or in part, or stored in a retrieval system,
or transmitted in any form or by any means, electronic, mechanical, photocopying, recording,
or otherwise, without written permission of the publisher.
For information regarding permission, write to Capstone Press,
151 Good Counsel Drive, P.O. Box 669, Dept. R, Mankato, Minnesota 56002.
Printed in the United States of America

Books published by Capstone Press are manufactured with paper
containing at least 10 percent post-consumer waste.

Library of Congress Cataloging-in-Publication Data
Polydoros, Lori, 1968–
    Anacondas : on the hunt / by Lori Polydoros.
    p. cm. — (Blazers. Killer animals)
    Includes bibliographical references and index.
    Summary: "Describes anacondas, their physical features, how they hunt and kill, and their
role on the ecosystem" — Provided by publisher.
    ISBN 978-1-4296-3390-1 (library binding)
    1. Anaconda — Juvenile literature. I. Title. II. Series.
QL666.O63P65 2010
597.96'7 — dc22   2009000950

Editorial Credits
Christine Peterson, editor; Kyle Grenz, set designer; Bobbi J. Wyss, book designer;
    Svetlana Zhurkin, media researcher

Photo Credits
Getty Images/Dorling Kindersley/Laura Wickenden, cover; National Geographic/Ed George, 8;
    Taxi/Brian Kenney, 4–5
Nature Picture Library/Nick Gordon, 28–29
Peter Arnold/Biosphoto/Luis Casiano, 18–19, 24–25; Tony Crocetta, 15; Martin Wendler, 22–23;
    TUNS, 16–17
Photoshot/Bruce Coleman/Erwin and Peggy Bauer, 12–13, 20–21; Wolfgang Bayer, 7, 10–11
Shutterstock/Dr. Morley Read, 26–27

TABLE OF CONTENTS

STRIKE!

The sun sets in the Amazon **rain forest** of South America. An opossum walks up to a stream to take a drink. Above the water, a huge anaconda waits silently in a tree.

rain forest – a thick forest where a great deal of rain falls

Suddenly, the anaconda strikes. It sinks its teeth into the animal. The snake wraps around its **prey** and squeezes. The opossum soon dies. The snake swallows its prey headfirst.

prey – an animal hunted by another animal for food

KILLER FACT

Anacondas have 100 sharp teeth inside their mouths.

BUILT TO HUNT

Anacondas are the heaviest snakes in the world. Females are bigger than males. Female anacondas weigh up to 300 pounds (136 kilograms). Males weigh up to 80 pounds (36 kilograms).

KILLER FACT

Female anacondas can be 20 feet (6 meters) long.

Anacondas belong to a group of snakes called **constrictors**. These hunters use powerful muscles to squeeze prey.

constrictor – a kind of snake that wraps around and squeezes its prey

KILLER FACT

Anacondas eat fish, turtles, crocodiles, dogs, and even sheep!

An anaconda can fit the head of a large animal inside its mouth. A flexible muscle connects the snake's upper and lower jaws. This muscle allows the jaws to open extra wide.

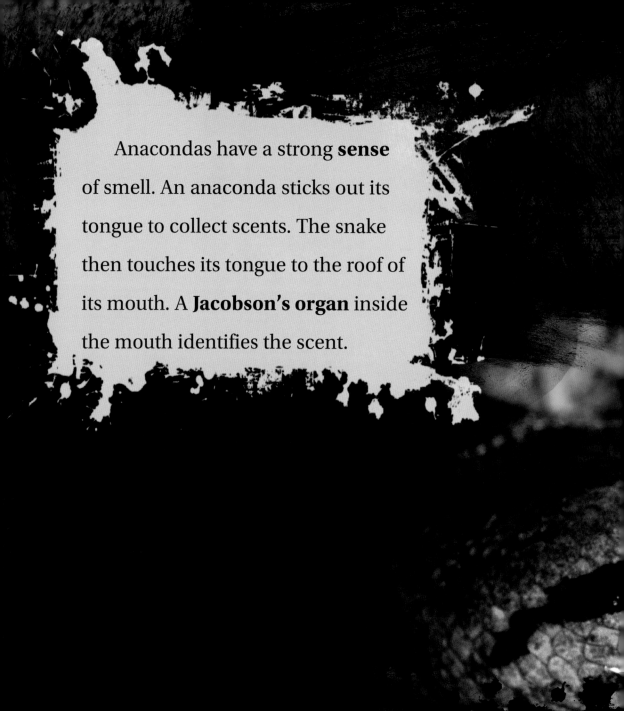

Anacondas have a strong **sense** of smell. An anaconda sticks out its tongue to collect scents. The snake then touches its tongue to the roof of its mouth. A **Jacobson's organ** inside the mouth identifies the scent.

sense – a way of knowing about your surroundings

Jacobson's organ – an organ on the roof of a snake's mouth that helps identify scent

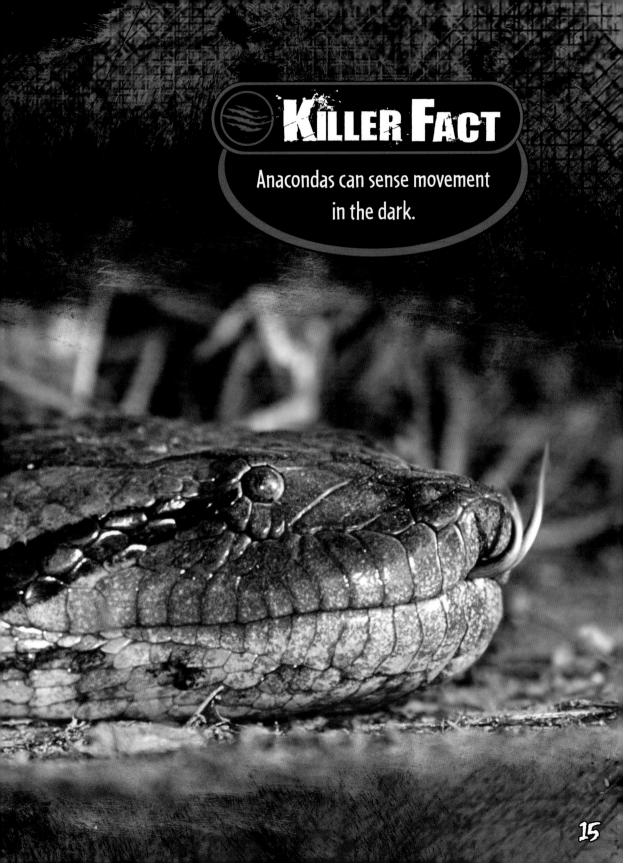

KILLER FACT

Anacondas can sense movement
in the dark.

THE SQUEEZE OF DEATH

An anaconda flicks its tongue in the air to find prey. It senses an animal nearby. Anacondas move quietly on land and in water. This smooth movement helps them sneak up on prey.

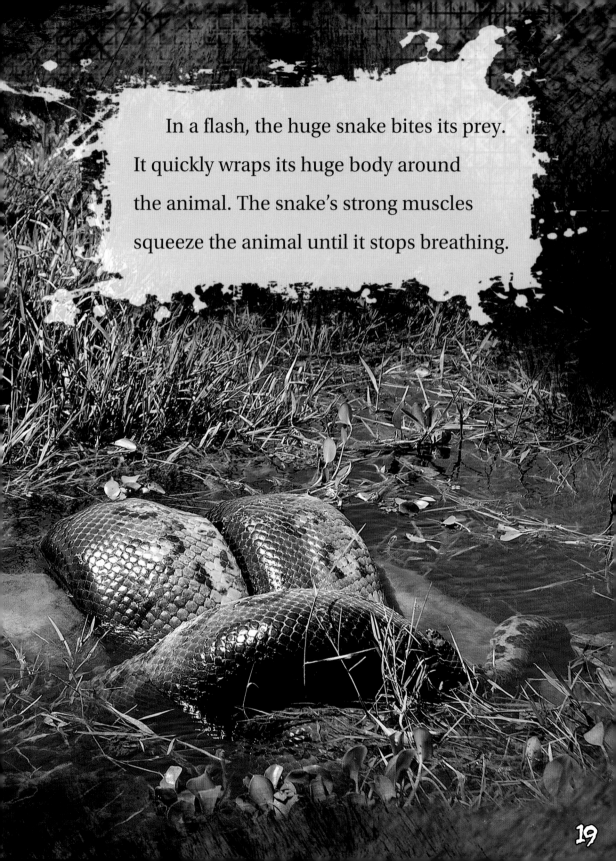

In a flash, the huge snake bites its prey. It quickly wraps its huge body around the animal. The snake's strong muscles squeeze the animal until it stops breathing.

Anacondas stretch open their jaws and swallow prey whole. Strong body muscles push large prey into the snake's stomach.

KILLER FACT

After a big meal, anacondas may go up to a year without eating again.

Anaconda Diagram

wide mouth

BALANCING THE ECOSYSTEM

Anacondas are part of a healthy **ecosystem**. They hunt both animals that eat plants and animals that eat other animals. Anacondas help keep the ecosystem in balance.

ecosystem – a group of animals and plants that work together with their surroundings

Anacondas do not eat humans, but people can harm this huge snake. People hunt anacondas and destroy their **habitat**. People must protect this heavyweight snake.

habitat – the place and natural conditions in which a plant and animal lives

KILLER FACT

Some people hunt anacondas
for their skins.

Ready to Strike!

GLOSSARY

constrictor (kuhn-STRIK-tur) — a type of snake that wraps around its prey and squeezes

ecosystem (EE-koh-sis-tuhm) — a group of animals and plants that work together with their surroundings

habitat (HAB-uh-tat) — the place and natural conditions in which a plant and animal lives

Jacobson's organ (JAY-kuhb-suhnz OR-guhn) — an organ on the roof of the mouth of a reptile that helps identify scents

prey (PRAY) — an animal hunted by another animal for food

rain forest (RAYN FOR-ist) — a thick forest where a great deal of rain falls

sense (SENSS) — a way of knowing about your surroundings

READ MORE

De Medeiros, James. *Anacondas.* Amazing Animals. New York: Weigl, 2009.

Mattern, Joanne. *Anacondas.* Snakes. Mankato, Minn.: Capstone Press, 2009.

Smith, Molly. *Green Anaconda: The World's Heaviest Snake.* SuperSized! New York: Bearport, 2007.

INTERNET SITES

FactHound offers a safe, fun way to find Internet sites related to this book. All of the sites on FactHound have been researched by our staff.

Here's all you do:

Visit *www.facthound.com*

FactHound will fetch the best sites for you!

INDEX